THE REVELATION
OF THE PROVERBS 31 MAN

THE REVELATION
OF THE PROVERBS 31 MAN

UNFOLDING THE PROPHECY OF PROVERBS 31

UNDERSTANDING HOW "HER HUSBAND IS
KNOWN IN THE GATES, WHEN HE SITS
AMONG THE ELDERS OF THE LAND."
PROVERBS 31:23

VAN BROWN

© 2007, 2011 by Van Brown. All rights reserved.
2nd Printing 2014.

Trusted Books is an imprint of Deep River Books. The views expressed or implied in this work are those of the author. To learn more about Deep River Books, go online to www.DeepRiverBooks.com.

No part of this publication may be reproduced, stored in a retrieval system or transmitted in any way by any means—electronic, mechanical, photocopy, recording or otherwise—without the prior permission of the publisher, except as provided by USA copyright law.

The author of this book has waived a portion of the publisher's recommended professional editing and proofreading services. As such, any related errors found in this finished product are not the responsibility of the publisher.

Unless otherwise noted, all Scriptures are taken from the *Holy Bible, New International Version*®, *NIV*®. Copyright © 1973, 1978, 1984, 2011 by Biblica, Inc.™ Used by permission of Zondervan. All rights reserved worldwide. www.zondervan.com

Scripture references marked KJV are taken from the *King James Version* of the Bible.

Scripture references marked NASB are taken from the *New American Standard Bible*, © 1960, 1963, 1968, 1971, 1972, 1973, 1975, 1977 by The Lockman Foundation. Used by permission.

ISBN 13: 978-1-63269-169-9
Library of Congress Catalog Card Number: 2007903066

TABLE OF CONTENTS

Proverbs 31:1,10-31 vii

Preface ix

Chapter 1: The Vision 11

Chapter 2: Not By Might, Nor By Power 17
    King David
    King Solomon

Chapter 3: The Lord's Maidens 25

Chapter 4: By My Spirit 33
    Impartations
    Calling Us to Virtue

Chapter 5: The Needful Thing 43
    Sitting at the feet of Jesus involves

Chapter 6: Giving Her Something Good to Study 51
    Making Her Know That She Is Greatly Value
    Entrepreneurism
    My Prayer For You
    The 25th Hour
    When You Hear Me Crying

Prayer Is The Key
The Dilemma
I Am A Ministry
The Angels Shout, Hallelujah!
Walking In The Law Of The Spirit
You Are My Epistle

Proverbs 31:1, 10-31

¹The words of king Lemuel, **the prophecy that his mother taught him.**
¹⁰**Who can find a virtuous woman?** for her price is far above rubies.
¹¹The heart of her husband doth safely trust in her, so that he shall have no need of spoil.
¹²She will do him good and not evil all the days of her life.
¹³She seeketh wool, and flax, and worketh willingly with her hands.
¹⁴She is like the merchants' ships; she bringeth her food from afar.
¹⁵She riseth also while it is yet night, and giveth meat to her household, and a portion to her maidens.
¹⁶She considereth a field, and buyeth it: with the fruit of her hands she planteth a vineyard.
¹⁷She girdeth her loins with strength, and strengtheneth her arms.
¹⁸She perceiveth that her merchandise is good: her candle goeth not out by night.
¹⁹She layeth her hands to the spindle, and her hands hold the distaff.
²⁰She stretcheth out her hand to the poor; yea, she reacheth forth her hands to the needy.

²¹ She is not afraid of the snow for her household: for all her household are clothed with scarlet.
²² She maketh herself coverings of tapestry; her clothing is silk and purple.
²³ **Her husband is known in the gates, when he sitteth among the elders of the land.**
²⁴ She maketh fine linen, and selleth it; and delivereth girdles unto the merchant.
²⁵ Strength and honour are her clothing; and she shall rejoice in time to come.
²⁶ She openeth her mouth with wisdom; and in her tongue is the law of kindness.
²⁷ She looketh well to the ways of her household, and eateth not the bread of idleness.
²⁸ Her children arise up, and call her blessed; her husband also, and he praiseth her.
²⁹ Many daughters have done virtuously, but thou excellest them all.
³⁰ Favour is deceitful, and beauty is vain: but a woman that feareth the LORD, she shall be praised.
³¹ Give her of the fruit of her hands; and let her own works praise her in the gates.

Preface

Before we begin I'd like to point out that it is very important to understand that Proverbs 31 and particularly the passage of scripture surrounding this great woman of virtue is **a prophetic teaching that has to be received as a prophecy.**

Commonly when we hear or read prophecy, we perceive it as something that will unfold and come to fruition that one time. But this particular prophecy is a perpetual prophecy that pertains to everyone that lends himself to it or waits on it. To wait on it is to apply one's heart and self to it. Anyone who receives this prophetic teaching and applies himself to it, working out the mechanics of it, can attain the promises of Proverbs 31.

The prophecy of the virtuous woman is about perfecting oneself to the point where others around you are perfected through your example of getting perfected.

I arrived at this premise for Proverbs 31 by an understanding, first, of Verse 1 which clearly states that this is a prophecy that Lemuel's mother taught him. Second, through the opening up of the word "find" which in Hebrew is the word "matsa." And third, through an understanding of why and how her husband is qualified to sit among the elders (counselors and decision-makers) of the land.

A Proverbs 31 Man is a true Christ-like leader. He has grown in virtue in many areas of life through his relationship with God, and his faithful following and gleaning from others who excel in the different areas that he's been trying to grow in.

He understands that God has put certain people in his life and in close proximity to him, and given him influence with them so that he can demonstrate and impart virtue to them and patiently help them bring that virtue to the forefront.

There are a multitude of examples of people mentoring and disciplining others to higher levels, but it is very rare to find people teaching, mentoring or disciplining with that Christ-like determination and focus that makes them demonstrate and impart virtue into the people that God has given them influence with, and later call those people to "glory and virtue" (II Peter 1:3)

A Proverbs 31 Man is received as a gifted leader by other leaders in places where they make decisions, because they can see his works in the people that are close to him. As you read this book, I encourage you to be mindful of the ministries of Jesus the Christ that are exemplified throughout these pages, and understand how Jesus is our first and quintessential Proverbs 31 Man.

Chapter 1

THE VISION

Lying before the Lord one day, I was reading the 31st chapter of the book of Proverbs. I wasn't studying it or trying to unlock anything heavy, I was just leisurely laying before God, reading the scriptures. The Lord began to open the word up in a radically new way for me.

I began to see more clearly the husband of the woman of Proverbs 31, who epitomizes virtue, and to understand how Proverbs 31 is as much about him as it is about her. By the end of this book we will have gained prophetic insight into the reason her husband is known in the gates, when he sits among the leaders of the land.

I believe that one of the most overlooked truths about Proverbs 31 is our grasping that it is a prophecy, and as such it must be opened and unfolded until one begins to see the mysteries of God. As the Spirit of God takes you deeper into the prophetic teaching of Proverbs 31 you see the work of Christ powerfully manifested and the true riches that God has for you.

As the Lord began to open this up for me, I envisioned King Lemuel's mother running her fingers through her son's hair, while trying to impart wisdom in ruling, leadership, and in being a valiant man. I envisioned her ministering the prophetic teaching of Proverbs 31, "Who can find a virtuous woman?" She wasn't ministering it from the perspective of "What qualities to look for, when considering a wife", but she was teaching it from the point of view that shifts the weight and pressure from the woman, whom we have foolishly assumed should "already" be this perfected woman before we marry her. The weight of the prophetic teaching is shifted to the men, whose leadership abilities, and readiness to handle such an awesome responsibility is called into question. A responsibility much like that given to men and women of God who stand and operate within the five-fold ministry offices, and have the responsibility of perfecting the saints for the work of ministry.

Some scholars hold King Lemuel, of Proverbs 31, and King Solomon to be the same person, citing that Lemuel is another of Solomon's endearing names. Many scholars dismiss this possibility, hugely because they hold the mother of Solomon, Bath-Sheba, as being disqualified to teach him this prophecy of a virtuous woman. I believe that so many people miss what God is saying here because it's not the prophecy of the virtuous woman, but the prophetic teaching of being able to bring forth a virtuous woman.

If the woman who is ministering this prophetic teaching isn't Bath-Sheba, then who is this woman that is in such fellowship with our God, and who is her son, Lemuel, whose name indicates one who especially belongs to God? I believe with scholars, who are of the school of thought that King Lemuel and King Solomon are one in the same. I believe that if it weren't for the sordid beginning of Bath-Sheba's relationship with King David, scholars would be bending over backwards to prove that Bath-Sheba ministered this teaching to her son.

I challenge you to do a survey, asking ten Bible thumpers the question "What's the first thing that comes to mind when you think about Bath-Sheba?" Then ask ten others "What's the first thing you think of when you consider King David?" I guarantee you the results will be overwhelmingly negative for Bath-Sheba, but overwhelmingly positive for David. Without a doubt, we are more forgiving of men than we are of woman, but God forgives us equally.

The Vision

I don't believe, that the prophetic teaching of Proverbs 31 was ministered by a woman who had attained such a level of greatness, but by someone who had been on the other side of the spectrum, a wretch, a woman who had lost what little virtue she had. And God, who has a way of meeting us at our bottom and causing us to see ourselves, then gives us a vision to help us get up. This woman was brought to a place where she could now see how she should have been, and began her journey on that course. A woman who would one day step up to the plate for her son, who should be king, at great risk of losing her life and the life of her son, by Adonijah, David's eldest son, who was showing himself to be the new king. Bath-Sheba goes in to David and reminds him of his word concerning Solomon sitting on his throne.

Bath-Sheba came through for her son so virtuously, that he acknowledges her as being instrumental in him being king, saying in the Song of Solomon, "Behold King Solomon with the crown wherewith his mother crowned him". Bath-Sheba had a vision. The woman ministering the teaching of the virtuous woman had a vision of the God kind of leadership. The kind of leadership that consistently demonstrates virtue, imparts virtue, and helps to bring virtue forth in others. She ministered the virtuous woman of Proverbs 31 being the end result of true godly leadership.

As she teaches the prophecy, she asks a question that for generations has been read over quickly to get to what we believe are the good parts, but the question itself, "Who can find a virtuous woman?" is where the power of God is for us. This question is akin to the counsel of Proverbs 18:22 that teaches, "Whoso findeth a wife findeth a good thing". Many people grow frustrated in their marriages because they approach this proverb, and the question of Proverbs 31 lazily, or faint heartedly, not taking the time to open these proverbs to understand the mechanics of them.

Don't you think it was rather foolish of us to think that to obtain favor from the Lord, all we had to do is acquire wives, and what about simply looking for that already perfected wife of Proverbs 31?

Men of old got into a lot of trouble because they failed to consider the whole counsel of God. Samson learned a hard lesson of betrayal in trusting his Timnite wife before imparting trust into her. Ahab got into all kinds of trouble with Jezebel, and Zeresh, the wife of Haman, designed his death by giving him evil counsel. Even in the book of Proverbs there is an account of a loud, stubborn, and adulterous woman who brings a young man into her and her husband's house while the husband is away. She was the cause of much pain and anguish, even causing her husband to bloody his hands in killing the young man.

All of these women were wives, but obviously they were not "a good thing". Does that make the word of God untrue? Not for a second. Those husbands, to their hurt, failed to press into the Christ kind of leadership. They, like most men today, failed to open up and understand the principals of "FINDING" a wife and a good thing, or "FINDING" a virtuous woman. The words "find" and "findeth", from Proverbs 18:22 and 31:10, are from the Hebrew word "Matsa", pronounced "mawsaw". In addition to carrying the meaning ~to lay hold of something or to acquire something, it also carries the meaning ~to bring something forth or to cause something to come forth. When we look at those verses from this perspective, they look more like this: "Whoso brings forth a wife, brings forth a good thing, and obtains favor from the Lord". And, "Who can bring forth a virtuous woman?" From this perspective, the weight is taken from the women, and placed where it should have been all the time, on the man, who is supposed to be the head and leader of his family.

Today, we live in a super fast generation, where we look for the quickest and easiest way in everything. We're getting so lazy. We are not completely lazy yet, because there are some areas in our lives where we'll sweat bullets, like in our careers and hobbies, however, we've adopted the idea that something as important as marriage should be easy, and readying oneself for it is no big deal. A couple of pre-marriage counseling sessions, and a couple of tear jerking confessions, and you're ready for your "good thing".

The Vision

If we continue to approach something as faithful as the responsibility of another soul so foolishly, just like the men of old, we are going to continue to see a whole lot of trouble. People we love will be hurt and their purposes will fail because we fail to "impart and bring forth virtue" in them, because we fail to understand the Christ kind of leadership.

Chapter 2

NOT BY MIGHT, NOR BY POWER

God is so awesome in His manifold wisdom, it is no wonder the angels praise Him twenty-four/seven. There is not a time when some facet of His wisdom and power is not being made manifest. Not only in our strength, but also equally in our weakness. I have seen Him so many times allow the shortcomings of one, to be a moment of visitation, an opportunity for growth to another.

He gives us gifts and talents and guides us to the areas where He's purposed us to be a part, to work our knowledge and gifts effectively to impact and give increase to the place and people He connects us with. Because you had to be there to give an increase, means that there was a need there. Not that gifts and talents weren't there already, somebody just needed your touch. And, God works in all of this to take us to new levels, revealing more of His glory.

KING DAVID

The Spirit of the Lord was upon David mightily. God had equipped him with skill and cunning, with gifts that brought him before great men. God was with him for victory; God was with him in fellowship, challenging and sharpening, encouraging and comforting. The Spirit of the Lord was on David to sing exactly the songs God wanted to hear, when He wanted to hear it. He worshipped God before heaven and men. He was truly a man after God's own heart.

But as awesome a man of God as David was, he had areas of shortcomings. The one shortcoming in particular that we're going to glean from is his "leadership towards women". Many people might say that "David was a great leader, he just had that one issue of lust with Bath-Sheba". I couldn't count the number of sermons that represented David's problem in that light, but let's launch out a little deeper. Other than a beautiful woman whose bath was situated where David could see her from his roof, who was Bath-Sheba? To King David, she was a subject under his rule, under his care and protection. She was like a daughter. In the Body of Christ, she would be a member of a mega-church, whose husband was working and even heading up one of the churches ministries. She is in awe of "Pastor David", the very charismatic leader who kills giants and destroys demons. He is a sparkling musician, singer and songwriter. When he speaks everybody is inspired and he has her brought in before him.

Now, no one will dispute that she should've said "No", and if she did say no she should've kept on saying it. I'll not exhaust all the different power plays, and head games that could've transpired. I am going to suffice it to say that Bath-Sheba had a major part in the wrongness of this event, and the related ones to follow.

But for a little while I ask you to look at this from the perspective of leadership, from God's headship principals. When viewed from here, no matter how out of line Bath-Sheba was, David's responsibility was to stand as a father, a protector of her, and her virtue. As a leader, just as towards the sheep, he should've guarded her, and reached out even to save her virtue. He should have covered her with Godly leadership. He watered and fed the sheep, so that they would be healthy and grow. What about people under his care? Now, no one would dispute that for the most part, David was virtuous. One of the most virtuous things for me was when I saw him using great restraint when he had the opportunity to kill the man that was trying to kill him, and to come into his kingdom. He abdicated his natural right

Not By Might, Nor By Power

to kill King Saul, and to ride in victory as the new King. He demonstrated great virtue there and in many other areas, like his sense of fairness, his obedience and his relationship with God. David was very virtuous, but as virtuous as he was, he was not virtuous enough to impart it in his neighbor, Bath-Sheba, who was under his care. He wasn't able to protect the little that she had already. He wasn't able to nurture it and help it grow. David could not "bring forth" virtue.

What about his leadership towards his first wife, Michal? Don't dismiss her too quickly because she was the daughter of Saul, even though Saul gave her to David to be a snare. Michal loved David, but David was so consumed with his wars, his friction with King Saul, and finally his fear of death, that he forgot Michal in all of that. He left her to fend for herself through all of that. For us, David was a type and shadow of Christ to come. When Jesus came, He literally dealt with the same things. He had to deal with His wars, His friction with Satan and finally the threat of death. But, throughout it all, He ministered His relationship with God to His disciples, and He did it more passionately. He knew that His physical time with them was short, so He didn't leave them before time.

Michal loved him, and laid her own life on the line in helping him to escape Saul. And, he escaped leaving his responsibility behind. He failed to cover her and protect her. He failed to guard and protect her virtue. She was given to another man while David was out marrying other women.

David loved God and worshipped God, but he didn't keep Michal by his side and demonstrate consistently his love for God and the principals of worship. If he had imparted this virtue unto her, she would have loved to worship. She might have danced out of her clothes too! Instead, when she saw him worshipping the Lord, she ignorantly despised him, and he in turn, hardened even more against her and would not give her any children/fruit. He made sure that she was not fruitful. Throughout all of this, he could not see how much she needed him, his covering, his worship, and his leadership.

David could not bring forth a virtuous woman. When King David was on the run again, this time from his son Absalom, he took all of his servants, his whole household, even 600 men that came with him from Gath, Cherethites, Pelethites and Gittites, but he left ten women, his concubines, to keep the house. When one of David's servants came and said, "Your servants are ready to do whatsoever my lord the King shall appoint." David appointed that "Everybody even the strangers are going to flee, but I want to leave my concubines to keep the house." When Absalom came to the city he took over the house and the ten women, but even more, he took over the ten women publicly, "in the sight of Israel". Even with his children, he failed terribly, saving for the relationship with God that Solomon received. David did not impart the virtue he had.

He was a mighty, valiant man of God, who excelled in God's favor, but he could not "bring forth a virtuous woman".

King Solomon

There are some powerful truths concerning Godly leadership towards women, so as to "bring forth virtue" that must be gleaned from the leadership of King Solomon. His wisdom exceeded the wisdom of all men in the earth, and yet, even he could not "cause to come forth a virtuous woman".

Solomon had seven hundred wives and three hundred concubines who are going to bear witness to his neglect to lead them to that place where they could have been mighty in God. Some might say, "But those women were from ungodly nations", and that would be true, but it's also true that our God is well able to change the heart of man. King Solomon had proof of that fact in his blood, his great, great grandmother, Ruth, was a woman from one of those ungodly nations. And another embarrassing truth is that it wasn't a man that brought Ruth forth, but another woman.

I find it incredibly intriguing the strengths we have in some areas, and the utter weakness in other areas. With all the wisdom Solomon possessed, he still allowed his heart to be turned to other gods. Though Israel was commanded not to take wives from other nations, God did not judge Solomon for it. He judged Solomon for going after other gods.

As wise as Solomon was, he had to be a great thinker. If you know any great thinkers, you know that for the most part they're okay. They'll mentally work something until it can't be worked anymore, they love to explore and figure out new and strange things, and sometimes they'll lose themselves for days trying to unlock some mystery. In most cases they contribute so greatly, but every now and again you'll encounter great thinkers who go a little to far out there, sometimes way out into left field, and sometimes they don't come back.

Even with great wisdom, you have to set boundaries for the things we allow ourselves to entertain. When you are a big thinker it's very easy to go off in thought into areas where you could lose your perspective while toying too far or too long with other perspectives. We should be knowledgeable concerning what's outside of our circle, but many times in our thinking we have said, "I'll not even think about that any further".

As wise as Solomon was, he didn't use his wisdom to set wise boundaries and to keep them. He should have known when to turn the conversation when his wives discussed their gods, just as we should know when to change the channel or cut it off completely, or when to avoid certain people. Solomon was the one who wrote about what happens to the field and vineyard when the wall is broken down. If Solomon had set boundaries, when he reached them his wisdom would have cried "My daddy was a prophet / king who said my God is above all gods, He's the beginning and the end, so I'll think about it no further".

I've heard many preachers say, "Watch out for those 'Verily, Verilys', because something important is going to follow". God said in 1Kings 11:9-10, "I appeared unto Solomon twice and commanded him concerning this thing, that he should not go after other gods". God said that He went to the wisest man in the earth twice about it and he still didn't get it.

As I began to look into Solomon's relationships, God showed me how Solomon did everything "FULL OUT". It made me think about when I was in the Marine Corps, and how me and my buddies had a motto "When we work, we work hard, and when we play, we play hard." On the weekends, if we didn't have duty, we were a bunch of drunks and we weren't good for anything, good. But come Monday morning, we were inspection ready.

When Solomon worked on the temple of God, he did it full out. The average person that looks at the pattern and materials that went into the temple would probably say, "It doesn't take all of that". But Solomon was tenacious about every detail, not straying from any he sent far and wide to procure whatever piece was not native to his region.

When Solomon made offerings and prayer, he went full out. For a peace offering he sent up 22,000 oxen and 120,000 sheep, and prayed exhaustively in dedicating the temple.

On the flip side of that, when he was at leisure with his wives, he did that full out. He made his time with them, their time. I've spoken with many men from different Christian denominations that hold hard to their doctrine of time-sharing. They actually believe that they give 8 hours at work, 8 hours to family, and 8 hours to God. These men actually espouse a special kinship to King Solomon, so I'm inclined to believe that they've grafted that doctrine from Solomon's writings.

There are many authors and conference speakers that are experts on the subject of time management and prioritizing, Solomon was one such, and from the authoritativeness in which he shares concerning the subject, one would gather that he was the master time manager.

It was Solomon that wrote:

> To every thing there is a season, and a time to every purpose under the heaven: a time to be born, and a time to die; a time to plant, and a time to pluck up that which is planted; a time to kill, and a time to heal; a time to break down, and a time to build up; a time to weep, and a time to laugh; a time to mourn, and a time to dance; a time to cast away stones, and a time to gather stones together; a time to embrace, and a time to refrain from embracing; a time to get, and a time to lose; a time to keep,

Not By Might, Nor By Power

and a time to cast away; a time to rend, and a time to sew; a time to keep silence, and a time to speak; a time to love, and a time to hate; a time of war, and a time of peace.
—Ec. 3:1-8

There is a time and place for everything, but as wise as Solomon was, he failed like so many today to realize that God is the exception to that rule. We "Live" by the words that proceed out of His mouth, so God should be somewhere in our time all the time.

If Solomon had grasped that, his wisdom would not have failed him and nations would have been closer to God. The seven hundred wives and three hundred concubines would have turned from following their gods, and committed themselves to following the true and living God.

How could I make such a statement? Remember, the witness was in Solomon's blood, through his great, great grandmother, and if that was too far back, God sent Solomon another witness. Too many times we get lost in her gold and precious stones, but God wants us to know that the Queen of Sheba's coming from Ethiopia was not just a visit, it was a wake up call that went unanswered.

Now Solomon loved and clave to strange women from the surrounding nations, women from Egypt, and Moab, and Ammon, and Edom, and Zidon, and Heth, but he didn't allow them any part of his God. In 2 Chr 8:11 Solomon said "My WIFE shall not dwell in the house of David, King of Israel, because the places are holy, whereunto the ark of the Lord hath come".

In his wisdom Solomon had already prioritized his time and compartmentalized everything. God on one hand and his strange women on the other hand, so God sent a strange woman, not from next door, but from another continent. She's not coming simply because of Solomon's fame, but because of the fame of Solomon concerning the name of the Lord.

Solomon answered all of her hard questions, and told her all that was in her heart, showing her that nothing was hid from him through the gift that God gave him. When she saw the prosperity 1Kings 10:5 says, "There was no more spirit in her". She was overwhelmed.

Solomon wrote in Proverbs 11:30 "The fruit of the righteous is a tree of life; and he that winneth souls is wise." I'm convinced by the strange woman from another continent, that if Solomon, in all his cleaving to his women, had ministered to their hearts concerning the name of the Lord, he could have caused their spirits to leave them long enough to impart some virtue, and then cause it to come forth, but King Solomon did not "Bring Forth a Virtuous Woman".

Chapter 3

THE LORD'S MAIDENS

The premise of this particular chapter holds a special place in my heart because it brings back memories of when I first began my relationship with Christ. I was living in Fontana, California, and had been just recently born-again. I was enjoying my newfound relationship with God, but at the same time experiencing some trouble in my flesh concerning my old circle of friends.

We had all been in the same Marine Corps unit, and several of us had gotten discharged and remained in the California area. We all were a long way from home, so we were pretty tight, and that was very important to me.

After I got saved, I learned very quickly that I had to be more responsible with the time that I spent with my old friends, and the way that I spent it. An average day for us consisted of drinking several 40oz, smoking weed, sniffing coke, and looking for new girls to brag about.

I actually had to downsize my contact with my old crew. But in doing so, I began to miss and even hurt for the type of comradery to which I was accustomed to. I found that real fellowship was lacking among the brethren at church. I was received with the standard, "Praise the Lord" and "God bless you", but as far as walking alongside each other and showing themselves to be friends, there was a huge void.

Even when I would step out of my hang-ups about not fitting in, and try to be more extrovert, I knew that the brothers just didn't know how to receive me. It was always pretty awkward. I was hurting, and God knew it, until one morning in prayer it all came gushing out upon God. I prayed it up to God in words I understood, in other tongues, and even in groanings. In the midst of my crying out, God spoke to my entire being, and I was paralyzed with awe as He said, "I am going to be your friend. We're going to laugh together and we're going to cry together". From that point, I knew that I would always be in the presence of my very best Friend, and that anchored me to grow in Him.

In like manner, God has ordained that we have Godly leadership, nurturers and encouragers around us, especially in the persons of fathers and husbands. But sometimes they're just not there, but God has a way of working it out so that the void is filled. He demonstrated that awesomely with Hannah, the mother of the prophet Samuel.

Now Hannah was the wife of Elkanah a man of Mount Ephraim, who had two wives. The one was Hannah, and the other was Peninnah. Peninnah had several children, but Hannah had none, yet the scriptures say that Elkanah loved Hannah especially. When he divided meat between everyone, he would give to Hannah a double portion.

The Bible depicts Hannah as being heavy with longings to bring forth a child. There were such stirrings in her at times that she couldn't even eat, and all she could do was cry.

In doing some work for hospitals, I've seen women come in for counseling and to undergo procedures to become impregnated. Many times I've tried to comprehend the heaviness of their need, but I knew that as a man I might only scratch the surface of what they go through. But I have felt the stirrings and heaviness of wanting to bring something good forth, and there has been times when I felt impregnated with vision and the stirrings and heaviness sometimes seemed unbearable. There were times, because it, that I myself couldn't eat, and in like manner, all I could do was cry.

Hannah was heavy with it, and I believe that the stirrings were more moving because it was in God's divine plan to use the fruit of her womb to usher in a powerfully new era. Her wanting to have a baby took her through such a gamut of emotional and spiritual levels that she went from wanting to have a baby for Peninnah, who was provoking her sore because the Lord had shut up Hannah's womb, to a level where she just wanted to have one to give back to God.

When a person is barren and experiences the stirring touch of God's divine purpose, keep your eyes on her, because when so much ministry is going on the person that's watching is also brought to pivotal point where they could be taken to new levels of glory. You'll see the barren grab a hold to God, and press, fighting the good fight of faith until that vision is brought forth. Or you'll see a person wallowing in their barrenness trying to fill that void with everything, from sexual promiscuity, anger, and arrogance, to being a workaholic, an alcoholic, or other substitutions that people hold on to until they get help or die.

Either way, whether you glean wisdom from the positive or the negative, you're going to see ministry. Solomon said, "I went by the field of the slothful, I looked upon it and received instruction." Proverbs 24:30-34.

In times of stirrings, it helps to have someone beside you who can discern where you are, and someone who knows how to help you press into God. A husband in many ways is already a pastor, and like a pastor, he has to be able to lay before God concerning his wife. He should be able to pull wisdom out of the Spirit for his wife, and he better than anyone else should be able to touch and agree with her concerning her breakthroughs.

There is a spiritual principal among believers that says, "One could chase a thousand, and two could put ten thousand to flight." Scripture tells us that "God won't put more on us than we could bear", but within that promise abides the counsel that, if you can handle it, there is a chance that you might have to make warfare against it.

If you as a believer enter into the covenant relationship of marriage, in the Spirit you are now built to put ten thousand to flight. You're no longer just one that can simply chase a thousand, but you're two that have the power to kick out ten thousand.

If you and your spouse are not in agreement, and on one accord, don't think for a minute that you only have the thousand to chase; you still have your ten thousand to put to flight. I strongly believe that this is partly why the apostle Peter wrote, "Likewise, you husbands, dwell with them (your wives) according to knowledge, giving honor unto the wives, as unto the weaker vessel, and as being heirs together of the grace of life; THAT YOUR PRAYERS BE NOT HINDERED."

Hannah was married to a good man that loved her and provided well for her, he pursued God to average degrees, in that he went up to Shiloh at the appointed times to worship, so we could say that he was a good church-going man. In all of that, he just like the majority of men today, was not before God enough to discern the fullness of Hannah's condition, to be able to help her. He reacted to her need much like many men today would, saying, "Why are you crying? How come you're not eating? Don't I take care of you better than ten sons could?"

Today, it would sound more like, "Baby, you've got it made; a nice car, a beautiful home, and you know how much I love you, so stop worrying about all that other stuff. Many men today are not kingdom-minded enough to stand beside their wives like a spiritual Lamaze coach, and help her bring forth to fruition, her vision. I have actually heard preachers say to their congregations, "I know that God's got something for my wife, but whatever He's got for her, He'll have something greater for me". And sadly, I've seen how their wives remain stuck outside of the place where they should be walking in ministries that God has for them.

If Lapidoth, the husband of Deborah the prophetess, had that kind of attitude, the book of Judges would probably be written a little differently. Either Deborah would have been stifled, or God would have killed Lapidoth. But Lapidoth, whose name means, to shine as a torch, obviously didn't have that attitude.

One of the most powerful things that I see in the kingdom of God today is the way Dave Meyer, the husband of Bible teacher Joyce Meyer, stands beside her and powerfully supports what

God has called her to do. To me, like Lapidoth, Dave Meyer is a shining example of how we as men need to nurture and release our wives to shine for the kingdom of God. When I hear "Momma Joyce" talk about some of the things that she has been through, I can see her husband there giving her grace and encouragement, helping her to come forth.

There are many women who, just like Hannah, are experiencing the stirrings and pullings of God, and while their husbands are good men who love them, they're just not there spiritually to help them come forth. But also, just like Hannah, God can bring them forth to bless nations.

There are not many accounts in David's story where we read of him dialoguing with women, much less taking their advice, but one account stands out powerfully to minister hope to women whose husbands may be there physically, but in the Spirit they're dead. Abigail was married to such a man. The word of God says that he was churlish: cruel, stubborn, and hardhearted. A man who followed after his given name, Nabal, which means dolt, stupid, wicked and vile, a foolish person, a fool. In the Hebrew tongue his name is the same word that is used in Psalm 53:1, "The 'fool' hath said in his heart, there is no God."

Nabal was of the tribe of Judah. He had great possessions of sheep, goats, and land. But his on servants saw him as a son of Belial and knew that it was useless to talk to him. Nabal's foolish heart nearly caused his entire household to be slaughtered. After David had kept Nabal's shepherds and flocks safe while they were among them, David's men were a wall unto them both night and day, a time came when David sent men to Nabal requesting that he show David and his men a little kindness in giving them food. David even went as far to say, "Whatsoever cometh to thine hand". Not only did Nabal refuse him, but he also offended David by adding strong and degrading words, accusing David of being a run away servant.

When David's men came back and told him how Nabal responded, what begins to unfold is a perfect depiction of what I see happening in the Spirit when we're praying for a breakthrough. When the young men made their request and were denied harshly, they simply went back to the master and went over how the enemy responded. The master immediately told all his men to gird their swords on, and he girded his on too because he was coming to unleash vengeance upon everything that pertained to Nabal, nothing and no one would be left. David swore it with an oath.

I believe that when we pray and go before God about our situation, and get refused, it's not always that He is saying, "No" or "Not yet". The prophet Elijah prayed for rain and it didn't rain, but he didn't take it as a "Not yet". He prayed several more times until it did rain. When Moses went before Pharaoh and told him what God said, Pharaoh refused Moses several times. The timing of the prayer was right, but God just wanted to show us something about how He'll fight for us. There was even a time when Pharoah wanted to submit, but God wouldn't let him, because God wanted to show us how He'll come, and He came with vengeance upon Egypt. Sometimes God just want us to come back and say, "God they're resisting you".

In the case of Nabal's household, God raised up an intercessor, which stood powerfully between the vengeance of God and her household. Abigail came like the Holy Spirit, with counsel and gifts, she came prophesying, and David knew it was of God, for he said, "Blessed be the Lord God of Israel, which sent thee this day to meet me: and blessed be thy advice, and blessed be thou, which hast kept me this day from coming to shed blood, and from avenging myself with mine own hand. For in very deed, as the Lord God of Israel liveth, which hath kept me back from hurting thee, except thou hadst hasted and come to meet me, surely there had not been left unto Nabal by the morning light any that pisseth against the wall. So David received of her hand that which she brought him, and said unto her, go up in peace to thine house; see, I have hearkened to thy voice, and have accepted thy person".

Abigail saved her household. With power she acted in prudence and wisdom. She prophesied to God's anointed, and it didn't fall to the ground. God said that Abigail was a woman of good understanding, but who walked beside her and demonstrated great virtue, and imparted it unto her? Well, we know it wasn't her husband because he was a fool, dead to the things of God.

I believe that God set Abigail before us, particularly before women to reassure and comfort them in the promise that, even if we as men fail in our leadership towards our wives, God will bring them forth; He will raise them up virtuously to lead and save many.

Many men today are dead to the things of God, but there is going to come a season when, for the first time, they will understand what their wives' have done, how she has been fighting the only fight that really matters, without him by her side.

I pray that, unlike Nabal who, in finally seeing it, was so overwhelmed that his heart died and he became as stone until the day he died. I pray that husbands repent and lay before God, growing in Him until they get to that place where they need to be.

Chapter 4

BY MY SPIRIT

And I saw in the right hand of him that sat on the throne a book written and on the backside, sealed with seven seals. And I saw a strong angel proclaiming with a loud voice, who is worthy to open the book, and to loose the seals thereof? And no man in heaven, nor in earth, neither under the earth, was able to open the book, neither to look thereon. And I wept much, because no man was found worthy to open and to read the book, neither to look thereon. And one of the elders saith unto me, weep not: behold, the Lion of the tribe of Judah, the Root of David, hath prevailed to open the book, and to loose the seven seals thereof.

—Rev 5:1-5

That passage of scripture will always be relevant in my life because it reminds me that anything that is worthwhile or lasting, has to begin with Christ, who is the beginning and the end of all things. From that passage of scripture, God has blessed me to see many of the tryings and failings of man, the types and shadows that served their temporary purpose, but weren't sufficient to perfect forever them that were sanctified.

Hebrews 12:2 say "Looking unto Jesus the author and finisher of our faith". Now that's not limited to chapter 12 of the book of Hebrews only, but that counsel extends to every area of our lives. We ought to look to Jesus to be the beginning and the ending, the writer and completer of every area of our lives.

So, when I began to put my hand to this word concerning "The Proverbs 31 Man", I went first to the Author and Finisher of everything good, to see how adamantly He would speak on the subject. Immediately, I found that He spoke not only adamantly, but also extensively concerning this word. He began to minister to me through His word, how He Himself, is the first "Proverbs 31 Man", and how it is truly the plan of God to bring forth all men as "Proverbs 31 Men".

Through His word, I began to see how Jesus is our quintessential Proverbs 31 man, who came knowing the heart of God towards us. He knew where God wanted us to be. He didn't come assuming that His bride would already be at the zenith of everything that's virtuous, but He understood that He would have to roll up His sleeves to faithfully walk out the awesome responsibility of "bringing forth a wife" and "bringing forth a virtuous woman". He accepted the responsibility by stepping forth, knowing what He was getting into by answering for the first time, that powerfully prophetic question, "Who can find a virtuous woman?"

I have read books and heard the debating of preachers trying to be heard, disputing the church's personification in the Spirit as the "bride and wife" of Christ. As the people of God, we should be at a place in this dispensation where it should be incontrovertible that we, the church, are the bride of Christ.

The apostle Paul wrote in 2 Cor 11:2 "For I have espoused you to one husband, that I may present you a chaste virgin to Christ". The apostle John heard a great voice in heaven saying, "Let us be glad and rejoice, and give honor to Him: For the marriage of the Lamb is come, and His wife hath made herself ready. And to her was granted that she should be arrayed in fine linen, clean and white: for the fine linen is the righteousness of the saints". Rev 19:7-8

When I read the last part of verse 7, it makes me consider God's generosity in accrediting the bride's "readiness" to her. If there are any so-called believers out there who thinks that they can do anything of real worth without Christ, they have not received Him properly, and are in need of having a proper foundation laid. Though God who is rich in grace, don't mind putting his glory on us, He demands a level of maturity that prompts us to give the glory back to Him. We know that it is Jesus, who is helping us to make ourselves ready. He's helping to make His espoused wife ready.

There are many things that Jesus did, and is still doing, to help us make ourselves ready. One of the most powerful things that He did in helping us to ready ourselves is that He consistently and powerfully demonstrated the heart of God to us, showing us, without the slightest deviation, what God has for us, and how God wants us to be. He came as the perfect ambassador from one country to another, to reconcile the two. As an ambassador, He showed us perfectly, the benefits of being a part of His country and how to walk in those benefits.

Like a business man involved in the merging or take over of another company, He came in, auditing our company's holdings, our policies and procedures, and everything that didn't flow with the new parent company's mission statement was exposed and uprooted for being counter-productive and a liability. He didn't leave us pacifiers, or shy away from certain matters because they might upset us. He exposed every hindrance to the kingdom that He encountered.

He didn't deviate from His course by trying to show the guys that He was really down to earth and could respond to life just like them. He stayed on course, and that's what He meant when He said, "I sanctified Myself for their sakes". He was saying, I didn't just remain separated from things, but I remained separated unto the things that I was supposed to walk in.

When I was growing up, "sanctified" was considered something negative. My friends and I used to tease the children of parents who we thought to be sanctified. We equated being sanctified with shouting, or what we called "catching the Holy Ghost". We made fun of the way they dressed with scarves on their heads and long dresses all the time. We equated being sanctified with being poor because anytime we saw what we thought were sanctified people, they looked poor.

I believe that many people have rejected the kingdom of God because we fail to truly represent the kingdom. I've heard so many people, even leaders, justifying themselves after they have misrepresented the gospel of Christ, and people don't come in. I believe that many people feel that they have to justify their approach in order to maintain the "power" in which they do it.

Sanctification and holiness were sorely misrepresented when I was growing up. The churches that surrounded me just didn't have the revelation at the time that being sanctified meant to be set apart to God's purpose for your life. To not only be set apart to God's word, yes, His whole word, but also His counsel and promises for a specific area of your life, you sanctify yourself to that word.

While being sanctified to God, I live a peculiar lifestyle in that I do many things that were not commonly understood among people that are not sanctified to God. My praise to God, my shout, and my enjoying myself in the Spirit of the Lord are all a part of my sanctified lifestyle, just like doing the tootsie-roll might be a part of the lifestyle of someone who is not sanctified to God. Within my sanctified lifestyle, I don't have to wear a tie everyday, and my wife doesn't have to wear dresses down to her ankles if we don't want to, but at the same time, we do set ourselves apart to God's counsel concerning dressing modestly.

Jesus walked in a sanctified lifestyle. It wasn't about His clothes, or His shout, but it was about His purpose. He was and still, is set apart to His purpose. When we view being sanctified from that perspective, where it's not about legalisms, but about purpose and the accomplishing of goals, it then becomes more inviting.

Sanctification is about being responsible and staying focused. It's a very strong word that cries out "You need to enmesh yourself in this counsel of God". When a man or woman of God is leading a people, and they themselves are not sanctified to their purpose in God, you might find them touching any and everything. They are tossed here and there experimenting with everything, and many times they'll even touch and experiment with unclean things because they are not enmeshed in the thing that God has purposed for them. The effects of an unsanctified leader, is like a cancer. It spreads throughout the church, stinking up to heaven. If the leader is lacksadsical, the followers that are close to him will be also. If the leader is sinful, the followers that are close to him will be too. Jesus said it in Matt. 7:17-18 " Even so every good tree bringth forth good fruit; but a corrupt tree bringth forth evil fruit. A good tree cannot bring forth evil fruit." The Apostle Peter wrote that Lot was a righteous, and just man, a man who stood against wantonness and lowliness of Sodom and Gomorrha. Though Lot, like many believers today, did good in standing and speaking out against ungodliness, he opened the door wider and wider to the destruction of his family by not sanctifying other parts of his life to God. His family observed him as he willfully resisted the urgency of God. As the two angels of God urged him to hurry and leave, Lot lingered. When the angels told Lot escape to the mountains, lest he be consumed, instead of yielding to God's counsel, Lot overexerted his will to get what he wanted. The examples passed on to his wife and children, who in addition to seeing him preach against ungodliness also saw him not sanctifying himself to the will of God when he wanted to do something different. Thank God for Jesus, who never took a "flesh-break". He never wavered from His purpose, but he sanctified Himself for our sakes, demonstrating consistently and powerfully how to walk virtuously in God.

IMPARTATIONS

The wisdom of sanctifying Himself so that we could consistently see Him walking in the power of God was not just for us to see that He was sent from God. It was also to shake and awake some divine things in us.

When God made us, He made us in His image and likeness. And, though because of Adam we are born with a "dead soul nature", there is still virtue and glory deep within us waiting to be stirred, awakened, and called forth. It's buried deep within us like a sharp and polished sword within the rough iron waiting to be sharpened. Jesus' walking in all that virtue was like iron sharpening iron for us. While the people that followed Jesus saw Him walking in all that power, it became like when Elisabeth was saluted by Mary, the babe within her leaped and she was filled with the Holy Ghost.

When a man or woman of God moves out in the power of God, contrary to what people think, it's not so that they could look cute or great, or to gather more people to their church, but it's to strike something within you with that two edged sword, to stir and awaken some divine things in you, because there is greatness in you. Jesus did a lot of stirring. When He walked on water He was stirring, and when He fed thousands, miraculously He was stirring, and when He was making lepers clean and giving sight to the blind, He was stirring and awakening and calling up within us the desire and hunger to be more. He has such a way of bringing people to a place of wanting to be like Him, and wanting to do what He does.

One awesome principal of impartation is the stirring to a place of hunger to receive. God counsels us in 1 Cor to covet earnestly the best gifts. When you covet something earnestly, you go after it, you study it out, and you push some things around and out of your life to enhance your chances to receive it, and that's where God's got you.

Without realizing it, you've been wrestling with God. You've been making room on the inside to receive something good. Proverbs tells us "A man's gift will make room for him and bring him before Kings." Isn't it awesome the way our wanting to be like Jesus and do the things that He does, will cause us to make room within us for Him.

Some things that I say here may rub many leaders the wrong way because it goes against the political correctness and what's commonly accepted as church protocol. In many leaders "perfect church" the people that are connected to them and follow them, do so because they are charismatic, they move powerfully in the Spirit, the way that they open up the word of God is like no other, and the vision that they have is the most awesome vision in the city. This is what many leaders want to believe. I've even seen how some leaders get bent out of shape and even act as if they are being betrayed when they begin to realize that some of the people that are following them, really want an impartation of what they have. It doesn't matter that the followers have been serving them faithfully. It doesn't matter that those same followers have been laboring faithfully to perpetuate that leader's vision. All of a sudden those followers are selfish "jack-legged wannabe" preachers. Many of them get blackballed and stifled by the Ministry Network. All because somebody got his or her ego bruised. Their egos get bruised because they are more self-minded than Kingdom-minded. They can't see pass their church, their vision, and themselves.

We have got to understand that the Kingdom is bigger than our visions, and especially our egos. The Kingdom is advanced on earth as we effectively advance the visions He gives all of us. God is connecting us to visions that we're to be faithful to, but while we are being faithful to those visions He has purposed for us to receive impartations of gifts and ministries from the leaders through whom we serve. God is awesome in His manifold wisdom in the way that He takes what may look like one simple event or situation, and work many different ministries through it. When someone is following a leader earnestly to receive impartations of gifts and ministries, that person has to humble himself under the hand of God, serving God by serving that leader, like Joshua ministered to Moses, like Elisha poured water on the hands of Elijah, and like followers today faithfully serve men and women of God. Like Moses and Elijah, there are many different types of leaders with different personalities and idiosyncrasies that God allows to break up the fallow grounds within those followers, changing their hearts and making room for a mighty move of God.

When the disciples received that mighty move of God in the upper room, their hearts were primed for it. They had followed Jesus closely, they were stirred and awaken by the power of all that He did and taught. They were brought to a point of longing to do what He did and to be like Him, they were coveting earnestly the best of gifts. Acts 1:14 say, "These all continued with one accord in prayer and supplication." Their hearts were primed to receive the outpouring of God's Spirit, and they received it mightily. Jesus is still pouring out upon us today, imparting His Spirit that's full of gifts and fruits.

Calling Us to Virtue

> Grace and peace be multiplied unto you through the knowledge of God, and of Jesus Our Lord, according as His divine power hath given unto us all things that pertain unto life and godliness, through the knowledge of Him that hath called us to glory and "VIRTUE".
> —2 Pet 1:2-3

Jesus, our first "Proverbs 31 Man" is calling us to virtue. Now, if we couldn't be this virtuous Proverbs 31 bride, He wouldn't be calling us to virtue. But He is justified in calling us to virtue because He consistently and powerfully demonstrated virtue to us, He poured out His Spirit upon us, imparting gifts and the fruit of the Spirit into us, and now He's calling us to virtue.

Even now that we are at a place in the Spirit where He is calling us forth to virtue, He is still there alongside us and even in us, helping us to come forth. Wow! What a Proverbs 31 man, imparting virtue in us, stirring within us and alongside us to manifest virtue, and in Heaven at the right hand of the Father interceding for us, so that we'll receive grace to get up and keep coming forth.

Make no mistake about it, this isn't about us looking cute or looking like we've arrived, but this whole thing is about fruit unto God. God is expecting fruit, and this is not a light matter, but a very serious one. So serious that Jesus had to come from Heaven to show us how to walk virtuously. In Luke 13:6-9 He spoke this parable, "A certain man had a fig tree planted in his vineyard; and he came and sought fruit thereon, and found none. Then said he to the dresser of his vineyard, "Behold, these three years I come seeking fruit on this fig tree, and find none: Cut It Down; why cumbereth it the ground?" And he answering said unto him, "Lord, let it alone this year also, till I shall dig about it, and dung it: And if it bear fruit, well: and if not, then after that thou shalt cut it down".

This is a serious matter, and this book is a serious wake up call to come forth with virtue, and not just a little, but with enough to reproduce virtue in others.

Chapter 5

THE NEEDFUL THING

As awesome as Jesus is, and with all the power in which He shows the Kingdom, it will profit us nothing if we don't rise up within ourselves to be open to Him and receive Him. To receive Him in a way that we won't be shaken from Him.

The one needful thing is to establish us in Him firmly at every new level. To be grounded in His knowledge of that level for us, and in His affirmation at every level we press into.

For the purpose of this book, the Spirit of God illuminated two principles that are inclusive to establishing oneself firmly in Christ. They are: "sitting at His feet" and "resting your head on His bosom."

To truly be established in a thing, you have to receive it, and to truly receive anything of worth you have to apply yourself to it. To be a musician you have to apply yourself to receive the music, to be a Wall Street money man you have to first invest yourself into numbers and money, into that system and pace, so to receive that system.

Throughout the Bible we see examples of people who abode in the spiritual position of sitting at the feet of the person whom God ordained that they receive. Receive what? Receive their breakthrough to higher levels, to be more firmly established in their purpose in God. Joshua ministered to Moses, Elisha poured water on the hands of Elijah, Timothy followed Paul, and Ruth the Moabite humbled herself and listened. Following the instructions of Naomi she received for herself a good man who firmly established her in the genealogy of Christ. They all were established in their purpose because they took the spiritual position of "sitting at the feet" of the one from whom they were supposed to receive.

The premise of this chapter is pulled from Luke 10:38-42, where Jesus ministers to Martha, who is upset because her sister is sitting at Jesus' feet instead of helping her to serve. Jesus lets Martha know that Mary has chosen "that good part", which is the one needful thing.

There are many things that we will need in our lifetimes. Proverbs tell us to get wisdom because it's the principal thing, but Proverb goes on to say "and with all your getting (of wisdom), get an understanding. Jesus is the Understanding, He is the perspective from which we should view everything we pursue and do.

Sometimes we get so caught up in the things that we are supposed to be putting our hands to; we become so taken by the people whom we are supposed to be serving, and receiving from. We get so caught up until we forget that in all of these things and people, we are supposed to be trying to see and receive Jesus.

Jesus has called me to serve and to be a servant, but He doesn't want me to be so distracted with serving until I prioritize it above the "one needful thing". Martha was "cumbered about much serving", which is another way of saying that she was distracted by her serving. Jesus wants us to serve, but if we don't grasp the "Jesus" of it, we'll serve, and serve, and serve, and never truly be established at that level.

I know that Jesus connected me with leadership in the body of Christ that I am to humble myself before. I am to serve them and support them, and to take the spiritual position of "sitting at their feet" to receive the Jesus of what they are teaching. However, He doesn't want me to be so taken with that person that I stop seeking "the one needful thing", the good part; the Jesus of it.

I use the phrase 'the Jesus of it' in this chapter for an important reason. When I began this project I wanted to use the

The Needful Thing

phrase 'the Christ of it', but God began to deal with me about how His children are being exposed to so many things, people and speeches that look and sound anointed, that they are beginning to follow after many of them. These things that look and sound anointed make the people of God feel good in their flesh, but they are not the anointing. It feels very Christ, very anointed, but if you look and listen deeper than the feeling, you'll see that Jesus is replaced with pride, Jesus is replaced with self-gratification and other spirits, so it's not Christ, but antichrist. The Lord led me to tell His people that in all their serving, and sitting at the feet of leaders to receive, always seek and listen for the Jesus of it.

I love the fact that Luke phrased it this way; "sitting at His feet", because right away it confronts the pride issue within us. Many people miss out on going to their next level because of the pride issues involved in submitting to someone else. Many there be that go on to higher levels in the natural because they know how to look like they are sitting at the feet of someone, but in reality they're only perpetrating a fraud. We don't have to be overly concerned about this because God hands out promotions where it really matters, so though someone perpetrating a fraud may seem to excel in the natural, in the Spirit where it matters, they are brought low.

Sitting at the feet of Jesus involves:

1. Making time to hear Him–Just as Mary did:

In the midst of all the things that we put our hands to, like our jobs, our families, our hobbies, and even our serving, we have to allow Jesus to put everything within them in their proper place and to give us wisdom in dealing with them. Family, job, ministry and hobbies are all good things that we ought to have in our lives, but if we let them distract us from hearing from the Lord to keep them in order, they will begin to set themselves up as gods in our lives.

2. Searching the Scriptures—In Two Ways:

We should search the scriptures line upon line and precept upon precept, here a little and there a little for a perfect picture and understanding of Christ. He is throughout the Bible, from beginning to end. We should search the scriptures line upon line and precept upon precept concerning the issues and situations that raise up before us, and concerning the things that God is trying to bring us into.

3. A Prayer Relationship—Not Just Certain Times to Pray:

Proverbs 3:6 counsel us to acknowledge God in ALL our ways. This means that we should develop and abide in a lifestyle that sifts everything through the knowledge of God. There should always be exchanges between God and us. When we pour out to Him, He pours out to our spirit. 1 Cor 2:9-12 reads "But as it is written, Eye hath not seen, nor ear heard, neither have entered into the heart of man, the things which God hath prepared for them that love Him. But God hath revealed them unto us by His Spirit: for the Spirit searcheth all things, yea, and the deep things of God. For what man knoweth the things of a man, save the spirit of man, which is in him? Even so the things of God knoweth no man, but the Spirit of God. Now we have received, not the spirit of the world, but the Spirit which is of God; that we might know the things that are freely given to us of God."

God is just swelling up with goodness to pour out to you, but you've got to always be pouring out to Him, like deep calling unto deep.

We pray or pour out to God verbally, praying with understanding and praying in tongues, allowing the Spirit to cut through all the junk and pray the real matter. We also pray through meditating. As a matter of fact, we are almost always meditating, but very little to God. We meditate a lot of junk, we ponder and toil mentally with problems, and we see the worst scenario in many cases. We look at and listen to negativism and allow ourselves to make room for it in our hearts: the very same hearts that we are supposed to be guarding because out of them are supposed to flow the issues of life.

The Needful Thing

The Bible doesn't speak as extensively about Isaac, the son of Abraham and the father of Jacob, as it does his father and his son. As a matter of fact, it seems that Isaac led a reasonably uneventful life when compared to Abraham and Jacob, but his life was just as exciting and prosperous as theirs, only with less stress. When Isaac's wife, Rebekah, was barren, Isaac didn't go in to the maid and produce an Ishmael. Isaac entreated the Lord for his wife and she got pregnant.

I believe that Isaac's life flowed a lot smoother because he was given to "meditating" on the Lord as demonstrated in Gen. 24:63. Now, he had his share of obstacles and hardships, but because he reinforced his outlook through his relationship with God, his life is an example of one resting in God.

Another way to "sit at His feet" is through seeking and yielding to His counsel. We need to condition and discipline our hearts to know the counsel of God when we hear it and when we see it. If we read and study and meditate on the pure unadulterated word of God, the sincere milk of the word, nothing added and nothing taken away, we will establish a solid understanding of how God moves, how God responds to different things and what He says in all of our various situations. Through this a knowing and discerning develops, and even when you find yourself faced with a new situation or hearing something for the first time, that discernment will rise up and say, "That's God" or "That's not God".

The counsel of God is not limited to the written word of God. When you realize that a brother or sister in the Lord has a good flow in something that you're struggling with or something that you perceive that you need imparted into you, Jesus wants you to take the spiritual position of "sitting at His feet" by studying your brother or sister for "the Jesus" of what they are demonstrating.

God has given us pastors according to His heart, who are spiritual parents, and Jesus wants us to take the spiritual position of sitting at His feet by receiving what our spiritual parents are speaking into our lives because some things just won't be unlocked until we go through those in authority.

There are men and women of God, whom God has raised up as experts in certain fields; some of them flow fluidly and maturely with the gifts that God has given them in the healing field, some in the money field, some the evangelistic field, some the deliverance field, and many others. These men and women of God have been raised up to be a resource for the body of Christ. They write books, they are on television and radio, and they are experts in the various areas in which we struggle. God has ordained that we "sit at the feet" of Jesus by receiving from these men and women of God.

Sometimes the people of God remain stuck because they allow roadblocks, like their personal dislikes, or someone influencing them to not receive from resources that God has set up to be a blessing to the body of Christ. Personally, I'm not sure that I could've hung out with John the Baptist, with his eating locusts and dressing the way he did, but I do know that I would've listened to him and received from him because I want to be everything that God is calling me to be.

To truly be established in the different levels that God is calling us to, we have to "sit at the feet" of Jesus, and that involves us applying ourselves to several established principals of God:

1. Making time to receive Him
2. Receiving His counsel
3. Praying (verbally and meditatively)

Another important part of the "Needful Thing" is learning to lay your head on the bosom of Jesus. We need to make sure that we MATURE in that place in the Spirit where He baptizes us afresh and afresh in His love, His acceptance, and His reassurance. Two-thirds of the temptations that Jesus suffered were attacks upon His relationship with God such as subtle craftiness designed to make Him begin to question who He was in God when He didn't perform the tests of the devil. Some people would tempt God and perform the tests just to show Satan who they are, but Jesus didn't have to wrestle with Satan concerning who He was in God. He didn't even acknowledge the part of the temptation that questioned His Sonship.

Many of us today allow the enemy to maneuver around us and sideswipe us by putting his hands on what we're supposed to be doing for God, while we are stuck in a wrestle about who we are in God. A wrestle that we should have won, even, at the beginning of our salvation. Today, people are so dazzled by the meats of the word until they develop a spirit of pride against receiving the sincere milk of God's word. Many pastors are giving in to the worldly peer pressure of always having to teach some new revelation, but every believer has to be nursed and weaned on God's love and acceptance of them, and established in the confidence of who they are in God.

According to John 1:18 Jesus came forth from the bosom of God, the place where He was established in who He was in God. Today, we need to abide in the spiritual position of resting our heads on Jesus' bosom. The apostle John did it until he matured in his understanding of God's love for him. John grabbed hold to it and held on until he knew that he was "the disciple whom Jesus loved". (John 13:23, 19:26, 21:7, 21:20)

In Numbers 11:10-12 Moses is grieved by the weight of burden of carrying so many people. "Then Moses heard the people weep throughout their families, every man in the door of his tent: and the anger of the Lord was kindled greatly; Moses also was displeased. And Moses said unto the Lord, wherefore hast Thou afflicted Thy servant? And wherefore have I not found favour in Thy sight, that Thou layest the burden of all this people upon me? Have I conceived all this people? Have I begotten them, that Thou shouldest say unto me, "carry them in thy bosom", as a nursing father beareth the suckling child, unto the land which Thou swarest unto their fathers?"

Jesus literally invites us to rest upon Him, to cast our cares upon Him. He can bear us all because unlike Moses, He conceived us. The apostle John laid his head on the chest of Jesus, a place where he felt confident that he belonged. It's in this spiritual position where one feels that he can ask God anything and he'll receive it. It's on His bosom where we have to allow Christ to nurture us, or we'll find ourselves being used by God, but stuck outside of that level where He reveals everything to us.

Peter was highly favored of Christ, but he abode at a level where he felt he needed to ask John to ask Jesus about the secret things. It wasn't Jesus that favored John more than Peter, but it was Peter who kept himself at that lower level, and while most of us would sacrifice greatly to operate at the level on which Peter operated, Christ wanted him to come closer.

Peter wasn't just there for the feeding of the multitudes. He was involved in the work. He held the basket, he walked on water, he healed the sick and cast out devils, but he still felt like he had to ask John to go before the Lord for knowledge that he wanted. Because of John's confidence in his relationship with Christ, Peter felt that John could get answers where he couldn't, but the only thing that separated Peter from that more intimate level was a personal application of the revelation of the Lord's love for us. John personalized it and abided in it to the point where he could confidently refer to himself as "the disciple whom Jesus loves", and that's a needful thing.

Chapter 6

GIVING HER SOMETHING GOOD TO STUDY

This chapter is a culmination of key principles grafted in from chapter 4, the principles of sanctification, impartation and calling forth. This is where Jesus gets to rejoice because we, His disciples, are now demonstrating that we "get it". In Luke 10:21 when His disciples returned with reports of how they were faithful in demonstrating the power of God, He warned them about getting puffed up, but in His spirit, Jesus rejoiced because His disciples were walking in what He demonstrated to them.

The word 'rejoice' here is from the Greek word *agalliao* that means to exalt, to be glad with exceeding joy, to jump for joy. The idea of finally making Jesus "jump for joy" gets me excited! After studying Jesus, our quintessential "Proverbs 31 Man", we are now bursting at the seams for being so ready to sanctify ourselves to some good works. We are ready to consistently demonstrate the power of God, walking in excellence in the things that are set before us. We want to give our wives good things to study, so that we can impart virtue to them.

Jesus gave, and is still giving us good things about Him to study. He knows how to woo us, and how to excite us while keeping us on our course of purpose.

Today we have men that know how to woo and excite women, but all too often it's at the expense of those women being distracted from their purpose. That is why this topic isn't simply called "Giving her something to study" because we're already giving them something to study; it's just not always "Good".

This chapter focuses on the practical application of several virtuous attributes from Proverbs 31. As Proverbs 31 Men, we now sanctify ourselves, not just for ourselves, but also for the sakes of the people who are following us, especially our wives.

There are eight practical power points within this chapter, that were grafted in from that most awesome virtuous woman of Proverbs 31. Being a "Proverbs 31 Man" is not limited to these attributes, but in other powerful areas as well.

For our obvious limitations I am led to expound from the following topics:

1. Making her know that she is greatly valued.
2. Entrepreneurialism
3. The 25th Hour
4. When you hear me crying
5. I am a Ministry
6. The Angels shout Hallelujah
7. Walking in the Law of the Spirit
8. You are my Epistle

As you read and meditate on these topics, I strongly encourage you to consider the steps that you can take in walking in each of these topics. See yourself taking the steps into them, no matter how small those steps may seem. Network with other brothers and acquaintances from the secular that are involved in some of these topics. Put it on your calendar and purpose to do particular things on designated days. Like Mary, the sister of Martha, make time to sit at the feet of Jesus to learn and do these things.

I pray that as you are reading these topics you take ownership of these attributes. I charge you to know that you are NOT alone, but myself and others, who love you in Christ, and especially Jesus Himself, are touching and agreeing with you; for you to come forth walking in the power of these attributes and others as the Proverbs 31 Man that God is calling you to be.

GIVING HER SOMETHING GOOD TO STUDY

MAKING HER KNOW THAT SHE IS GREATLY VALUE

~HER PRICE IS FAR ABOVE RUBIES~

Jesus has consistently demonstrated the importance and urgency of showing your bride not only that you love her, but also that you value her greatly. The apostle John knew it and abode in it. Peter really began to see it after he denied Christ, when Jesus asked for him specifically to come to Him. I believe that Judas began to see it after he betrayed Jesus, and the weight of the revelation of his betraying this man who did nothing but show everybody love was too much for him to bear. Of course, the ultimate demonstration of how much Jesus valued His bride was His laying down His life in her stead.

We have to consistently be there for them, no matter what, demonstrating how much we love them. Before we look into the importance of showing them how much we value them and some of the ways we should do it, I believe it is vitally important to understand the limits. Yes, we have a limit, a clear line that we don't cross, not even for her.

1 Cor 7:32-33 tells us that "He that is unmarried careth for the things that belong to the Lord, how he may please the Lord: But he that is married careth for the things that are of the world, how he may please his wife".

While being married, God uses the husband and He uses the wife, and many times He use the two together in mighty ways. Here the apostle Paul is expressing how, without condemnation, God has made provision or weighted in advance that the obligations of marriage will thwart your availability to Him. The understandable need for you to give yourself to your wife understandably affects what you otherwise could be freed up to do for God. While your availability, and sometimes your intensity, may be affected because you love and greatly value your wife and marriage, you absolutely must not cross lines pertaining to Godliness and your salvation. While you may die for her, you may not go to hell for her.

You need to make sure that those lines are clearly understood, and you need to stick to it. While Samson did awesome feats to demonstrate how much he valued his women, he understood the lines that he should not cross. Though this mighty man of God resisted, he crossed that line and greatly jeopardized his relationship with God.

1 Tim 2:14 tells us that it wasn't Adam that was deceived, but Eve was deceived. From that I see that Adam made a conscious decision. Understanding that he was putting his relationship with God on the line, he chose to follow his woman. We'll not examine all the different explanations for Adam following his wife, but suffice it to say that just like Adam, we can take a Godly thing and hold it in an ungodly place. When we cross the line of our relationship with God for anything or anyone, we are in effect setting that thing or that person up as a type of god in our lives. That's a very dangerous place to hold anyone, but most of all it would be detrimental to our salvation.

Now, having said that, aside from my relationship with God, my wife is the most important thing ever to me. She's more important than mom and dad, than the kids. My career doesn't come close to her. Not even the things in life that bring me personal happiness. I choose her over everyone and everything else because I value her above them all.

Feeling it and saying it is one thing, and that's good, but with this particular species of God's wonderful creation, you have to show them the money! I'm talking about letting your actions speak for you. Even Jesus tells us, "If you don't believe Me, believe the works that I do, that you may know and believe."

Brother, you have to work the works of God. You have to be that "SHOWER", where God says in Ezekiel 34:26, "I will cause the shower to come down in his season; there shall be showers of blessing." From the smallest to the greatest, lavish her and make her head spin. Do it with words, but reinforce it with flowers when you haven't even done anything wrong. Do it with words, but reinforce it by preparing dinners even if you can't cook. Prophesy great things into her spirit, take her by the hands and touch and agree with her concerning those things she wants God to bring to pass. In your personal prayer time, entreat the Lord for her fruitfulness. In the midst of your busy life, discipline yourself to pause for her. Your making time for her is so important that God Himself yields to it. Consistently show her that you've got her back, when the world is against her, even your momma.

Her price is far above rubies, so show her that you are like Jesus, the first Proverbs 31 man, who said this and performed it, "Again the kingdom of heaven is like unto a merchant man, seeking goodly pearls: who, when he had found one pearl of great price, went and sold ALL that he had, and bought it." She has to consistently see how you value her because just like we need to lay our heads on Jesus' chest and be reassured that we are "the disciple whom Jesus loves", she's got to be able to know that she belongs in your bosom and she can trust that you are always for her. That's when she'll follow you anywhere.

Entrepreneurism

I use to be an enterprise, now I'm a conglomerate

This premise is born from Proverbs 31:13,14&16, where God demonstrates through this woman the power of entrepreneurism and the spirit of increase. God has been saying a lot about increase and we've been acting like we "get it", but now He's about to say more about increase and we had better get it because now it's about us receiving it to the degree that we impart the spirit of increase to others.

It's not enough that you know how to go out and win the bread. There are too many horror stories about husbands dying and leaving widows behind financially perplexed. It's not good enough that you can work deals and excel in your career, or apply your skills and gifts to ideas to gain your increase. Remember, it wasn't enough that King David worshipped God while his wife was judged because she didn't understand worship. It wasn't good enough that King Solomon was the wisest man in the earth if he failed to understand that he needed to impart true wisdom into his wives, who didn't know God.

There have been many wonderful teachings concerning increase by today's leaders in the faith, and I believe that a large segment of our Christian community has grasped the word of prosperity and have been faithful with it, but it saddens me to say that many of us have not received that word faithfully. Many of us are going to have to go back and be faithful with those principals of increase, so that we can couple those principals to what God is saying now, because it's no longer simply about you operating in increase. Now it's about you operating in it to the degree that you impart the spirit of increase into others, most especially your wife.

The virtuous woman of Proverbs 31 was very industrious. She had a vision of working with wool and flax, so she sought out her starting point and put her hands diligently to it. Because of her industriousness, her business grew and God began to stir up gifts for other areas of business. With the profits she made from wool and flax, she bought a field and turned it into a successful vineyard.

Jesus, our first Proverbs 31 man, consistently demonstrated industriousness. He was often heard to say, "I must work while its day". From His youth He would put His hands to the things of God, saying, "I must be about My Father's business". When He stepped out fully to do the work, He didn't just manage an enterprise, but He successfully operated several different ministries, shifting in different areas to reach all demographics. He was a walking conglomerate.

Jesus taught and demonstrated the principals of divine increase to us from A to Z. From taking baby steps to miraculously receiving needs straight out of the Spirit. He gave us an example In Matt 25:14-28 Jesus is teaching principals of divine increase that are loaded with powerful revelations. Matt 25:14-28 "For the kingdom of heaven is as a man traveling into a far country, who called his own servants, and delivered unto them his goods. And unto one he gave five talents, to another two, and to another one; to every man according to his several ability; and straightway took his journey. Then he that received the five talents went and traded with the same, and made them other five talents. And likewise he that had received two, he also gained other two. But he that had received one went and digged in the earth, and hid his lord's money. After a long time the lord of those servants

Giving Her Something Good to Study

cometh, and reckoneth with them. And so he that had received five talents came and brought other five talents, saying, Lord, thou deliveredst unto me five talents: behold, I have gained beside them five talents more. His lord said unto him, Well done, thou good and faithful servant: thou hast been faithful over a few things, I will make thee ruler over many things: enter thou into the joy of thy lord. He also that had received two talents came and said, Lord, thou deliveredst unto me two talents: behold, I have gained two other talents beside them. His lord said unto him, Well done, good and faithful servant; thou hast been faithful over a few things, I will make thee ruler over many things: enter thou into the joy of thy lord. Then he which had received the one talent came and said, Lord, I knew thee that thou art an hard man, reaping where thou hast not sown, and gathering where thou hast not strawed: And I was afraid, and went and hid thy talent in the earth: lo, there thou hast that is thine. His lord answered and said unto him, Thou wicked and slothful servant, thou knewest that I reap where I sowed not, and gather where I have not strawed: Thou oughtest therefore to have put my money to the exchangers, and then at my coming I have should received mine own with usury. Take therefore the talent from him, and give it unto him which hath ten talents."

First, I want to remind you that the "GOODS" are from God. The monies, the gifts, the talents and abilities, every purpose-oriented vision, idea and opportunity are EMPOWERMENTS from God that He is expecting an increase on. He expects us to advance the kingdom of God in different ways with the "goods" that He gives us according to our several abilities. In the above passage of scriptures, even the servant that was given one talent had several abilities to make an increase, or his lord would not have given him his goods. Observe how the servants with five talents and two talents went out immediately, and industriously began to work their abilities and the monies that were given them. Now, I want you to get ready to be blessed. After the master called them all in for a business meeting to receive an account of everyone's business activities, promotions were released. A new level in God was opened up to the two industrious servants;

they were invited to a "PLACE" in the Spirit called the "JOY OF THE LORD". Now, we know that God gives us joy that we are to receive and hold on to, but here Jesus reveals that there is a place that we can enter into known in the kingdom as the JOY OF THE LORD. It's in that place, the joy of the Lord, where God commands that there be a shifting of assets from the unfaithful to the faithful. This is demonstrated in verse 28 where the talent was taken from the servant full of excuses, and given to the industrious servant.

The joy of the Lord is more than what Jesus had. It is the place in which He abode. A place where wine could be manifested from water, a place where money could be found in the mouth of a fish, and a place where multitudes could be fed from two fish and five loaves. The joy of the Lord is where faithful, industrious believers abide because they are the "go-getters" concerning God's principles of increase.

Your wife needs to consistently see you being industrious concerning increase. Let her see you working your talents and interacting in business. Tell her your ideas and visions, and let her see you go after them. Let her hear you and see you close up in battle. She especially needs to see you working God's principles for increase, giving alms, sowing into the work of God. Let her see you being a blessing and let her see as God commands men to give unto your bosom abundantly. As a Proverbs 31 man, let your wife see you consistently abiding in the joy of the Lord, so that it can be stirred up within her to help her get to that place.

My Prayer For You

Right now in the name of Jesus, I touch and agree with you concerning that place in your heart that releases the issues of life. I call forth your creativity. Mountains, rocks and walls, and every hindering spirit that has been assigned to halt your prosperity, I command to bow in the name of Jesus. I command them to be moved from before the issues of creativeness that is within you. In the name of Jesus, I strike the sword of creativity within you with the sword of God and challenge you, my brother, to understand what God has put within you. I challenge you to step out on it and work it and rework it to give increase to the kingdom of God, which includes your house. I rebuke the spirit of procrastination and shout "Flee" to the spirit of slothfulness. To the gifts, creativeness, visions and purpose within you, I strike with the sword of the word of God, which commands you to "Be Fervent In Business". Creativity and vision leap up like a Spirit-filled baby within the womb. Gifts and purpose kick and stir my brother awake, shake him with urgency and stir him with zeal. Cause your carrier to make ready for your coming forth. I speak to the hands of my brother and declare that God has taught you to war, and your fingers to fight a good fight. In the authority of Jesus' name I command this so, AMEN.

THE 25TH HOUR

MAKING TIME FOR WHAT'S IMPORTANT TO YOU

In chapter 2 we examined King Solomon's leadership and took a brief look at his time management approach to life and relationships. We found that aside from God, king Solomon could be held today as the father of time management. We learned that while Solomon was a master of time management and compartmentalizing the different things in his life, he went overboard in separating God from his relationships. Though Solomon went overboard with his time management and compartmentalizing, God wants us to understand that those principles are still very important for us.

Many times we get so caught up in giving our time to the things we really enjoy, and even, to the things we consider monotonous that have to be taken care of. As men, we feel the full weight of responsibility for our family's success, and all too often we forget the little things; "the little foxes that destroy the vines". We forget, and sometimes consciously sacrifice, key times that have been ordained by God for us to be in a needed place, to speak into the lives of key people in our lives.

Ephesians 2:10 reveals that God created us in Christ for good works, which God has ordained from the beginning that we walk in them. No, we are not saved by our good works, but we are saved for good works, so it is very important that we be Spirit led in the things we give our time to. Yes, you need to bring home the bacon, but you also need to be sensitive to when you need to toss the ball around with your sons, when you need to take your girls out for a soda. One sure way to allow the enemy into the midst of your successful family life is to keep forgetting dates that your wife considers special. These may seem like light things, but they are a part of the ministry of being there, touching the things that you have been ordained to touch. Ephesians 5:15-17 in the amplified bible reads, "Look carefully then how you walk! Live purposefully and worthily and accurately, not as unwise and witless, but as wise-sensible, intelligent people; Making the most of the time- buying up each opportunity because the days are evil. Therefore do not be vague and thoughtless and foolish, but understanding and firmly grasping what the will of the Lord is."

Sometimes we can get so closed in and bogged down by the constraints of time, but as "Proverbs 31 Men" we have to reach for the likeness of our Father, who is Eternal. We have to get such a handle on time that it seems like we're on top of it. Our Father is eternal, standing outside of time while operating in time, and never bogged down by the constraints of time. He has time for every thing that's a part of His purpose, and He touches all of them, so that each would have, it's ordained time to receive an impartation from Him. We have His eternal Spirit within us, so we have the capability to be on top of our time.

As Proverbs 31 men, we should be consistently demonstrating to our wives that we know how to make time. When we need to accomplish something important, and when something, or especially someone, needs our personal touch, we know how to prioritize, we know how to move some things around. We'll sacrifice sleep if need be, and if it takes a 25th hour in the day, we'll make one.

When Martha was cumbered about with much serving, Mary made time to sit at Jesus' feet. The virtuous woman of Proverbs 31 made time to pursue her vision. Verse 15 proclaims that she

Giving Her Something Good to Study

got up while it was yet night, and prepared meats and took care of every other household responsibility she had, so that she would be freed up to put her hands to the vision she had.

Jesus, our first Proverbs 31 Man, demonstrated powerfully how He shifts and move things around to touch the things His Father ordains. In Mark 5, Jesus is going to the house of Jairus, a ruler of the synagogue, to heal his daughter who is at the point of death. All of a sudden He has to make time for a woman whose faith had just become a high priority. In verse 30, He turned from going to the house of the man whose daughter was dying to further minister to this woman whose faith commanded His time. Teaching faith was a priority for Him, so being on top of His time, He made time for her, and later raised Jairus' daughter from the dead.

As Proverbs 31 men, we need to evaluate the people and things in our lives, and the things that we should add to our lives. We have to realistically put them in their places of priority, and we need to shift between them wisely. We especially need to make sure that our wives see us on top of our time and not bogged down by it and dying of stress.

When You Hear Me Crying

> She girdeth her loins with strength, and strengtheneth her arms. She perceiveth that her merchandise is good: her candle goeth not out by night.
> —Proverbs 31:17,18

Anytime you step out to pursue your vision or to put your hands to anything of value, the world has a way of strategically setting obstacles before you, in the form of people and things, to discourage you. They come to not only remind you of your limitations, but to minister your limitations to you. It is a constant fight, but I thank God for letting us know that it's a good fight, even the "good fight of faith". When you've been dealing with people trying to take advantage of you and rejecting you all day, it takes almost everything out of you, and it takes strength to get up the next day and continue pressing.

The virtuous woman of Proverbs 31 doesn't miss a beat, but demonstrates that between pursuing her vision, working deals, and taking care of family and ministry, she sets a special time aside to take care of herself. She's tired but she doesn't allow her candle to go out before she strengthens her arms, or before she fortifies herself. Proverbs 31:17 tells us "She girdeth her loins with strength", so approximately a thousand years before it was written in a letter to the church, she had the counsel of God in her spirit telling her to "Stand therefore, having your loins girt about with truth". At the end of the day she encourages herself. She tightens the belt of truth around herself, the truth about what God called her to do, the truth about her "merchandise" being the best, and the truth that God would be with her. Someone imparted in her the principle of renewing oneself, so when she awakes in the morning she's ready to go.

Prayer Is The Key

If we are ever in need of an example of a particular type of prayer, I'm sure that most of us will agree that God has supplied it in His word. We have numerous examples of faithful prayers to God, from Isaac's meditating, to the publican's smiting his chest and crying, "Lord, forgive me, a sinner". From Elijah's praying "SIX" times for the rain to come, to Adonijah's grabbing hold to the horns of the alter and not letting go. From Hezekiah's spreading threatening letters on the floor that were sent to him and telling God that the letters were sent to God, and powerful prayer examples like Jacob's wrestling with God. If you're in a situation and want to see how others in similar situations called on God for help, it's in the word.

Our joy and strength flows through our relationship with God, particularly our prayer life. If you show me a defeated Christian, I'll show you someone who isn't being faithful in their prayer life. Our prayer life is vital to our well being, and as Proverbs 31 men we should be fluent in all forms of prayer,

Giving Her Something Good to Study

but remember, it's not good enough that you know how to go before God and strengthen your hands and encourage yourself. It's not good enough that you know how to lay before God and cry out to Him for affirmation, and to get girded up for round 2 the next day, but you have to walk so consistently in it and you have to be "sanctified" to it to the degree that others who are watching your life, especially your wife, will receive an impartation from you.

The Dilemma

From Jesus' teachings in Matthew 6 about doing certain things in secret, particularly making prayers, I believe that Jesus had to choose between praying in secret, which is the most effective, and demonstrating to His disciples how to go before God and strengthen themselves.

Jesus may have slipped off to pray all night, but He made sure that whoever was studying Him would know that He slips off at night to commune with His Father. Peter saw it, and John saw it. They saw it enough to know that they needed to know how to do it. I'm sure that Jesus rejoiced to see the fruit of His labor.

John said in Revelation 1:10, "I was in the Spirit on the Lord's day". He went so deep in the Spirit that some people today are still afraid to read about the things John saw in the Spirit. By himself up on a rooftop, Peter fell into a trance and received a vision that revolutionized his whole evangelism approach. Wouldn't it fill you with joy to know that if your wife is in a tight situation, she knows how to go into the Spirit and receive strength from God?

As a Proverbs 31 man, you have to consistently demonstrate that you know how to go before God, and you have to be like Jesus, our first Proverbs 31 man, and not just allow your bride to see you going to pray. Actually get her involved, and exercise her in it. Jesus challenged and exercised His disciples in prayer, telling them to stay up and watch with Him while He prayed. In Luke 9 He took them up into a mountain to pray, and they witnessed Him praying until He physically changed before their eyes.

As a Proverbs 31 man, you are mandated by God to disciple your wife in the different kinds of prayers. She must see you consistently being transformed by your prayer life to the point where she covets earnestly a prayer life like yours, a prayer life that encourages and strengthens her to get up and pursue everything that God has for her.

I Am A Ministry

We are living in the greater works era, and it is exciting. Faithful men and women of God have been teaching and preaching concerning vision and purpose, and that's stirring and challenging the spirits of believers. It's making them long to put their hands to the things of God, and be effective in the different ministries to which God has called them to.

2 Cor 1:3,4 encourages us to work ministries. "Blessed be God, even the Father of our Lord Jesus Christ, the Father of mercies, and the God of all comfort, who comforteth us in all our tribulation, that we may be able to comfort them which are in any trouble, by the comfort wherewith we ourselves are comforted of God."

God has filled our hearts with ministry. In most cases the very things that we are exposed to, and touched by, are the things for which we have great compassion. I didn't say in all cases because sometimes "men withhold the truth in unrighteousness; because that which may be known of God is manifest in them; for God hath shewed it unto them" Rom 1:18,19.

After Lazarus had experienced the stench of death and been raised from the dead by Jesus, he had a great opportunity to minister to Jesus against the day of His burying. Lazarus understood the stench and discomfort of death, but he simply sat there. The Bible shows us that Mary THEN took a pound of ointment and anointed Jesus, and comforted Him against the day of His burying.

I have heard many people reflect back on their troubled childhood and mention how they would always say, "When I have

Giving Her Something Good to Study

children, they'll never be treated like this". Some of them actually had children just to treat them better than they were treated.

We all have ministry in us, and Jesus showed us how to minister our ministries to people who will faithfully receive it. He showed us how when ministering our ministries, we should always point the people that we are comforting to God.

In Proverbs 31:20 the virtuous woman reaches into her gifts and into the place where she's comforted, and stretches out her hand to the poor and needy. She covers them with her ministry.

As a Proverbs 31 man, God's plan is for you to take your ministry to a higher level. You should already be ministering to the vision of your local church. You should be propelling your church's vision with all kinds of prayers, with your faithful giving. You should be ready to lift your hand, volunteering your presence and strengths to various departments and programs, especially the ones for which you have a zeal. As God increases you in knowledge and in anointing, you should be stepping up to be used by God to strengthen His people. You should also already be ministering outside the four walls of the church building. Just as Jesus sent His disciples back then to work ministries while preaching that the kingdom of heaven was at hand, Jesus wants you to be wise with opportunities that are brought. He wants you to work your ministry and preach that the kingdom of heaven is at hand.

Working your ministry outside the walls of your church is also a support to that ministry because while all of the fruit of your labor comes into the body of Christ, some of that fruit will remain at your local church. These are some things in which you should already be walking.

Now God wants to take it to the next level. He wants you to work it with such intensity and power that you impart it to your wife. As Christ walked His disciples through ministries and exercised them in it by training them and backing them, and just like your pastor should be doing with you, you need to "SANCTIFY" yourself to working your ministry. You need to disciple your wife in it. You need to help her develop her ministry, and supportively back her up, as she needs your support.

THE ANGELS SHOUT, HALLELUJAH!

Proverbs 12:4 say "A virtuous woman is a crown to her husband". She makes him shine, as her greatness is greatly accredited to him. The virtue that she walks in, commands that he be received as a king.

As a Proverbs 31 man, you've got to be faithful with what God is revealing to you. If you sanctify yourself to working the principles that you have been reading in this book, the power of God will loose your wife and propel her to new heights. When true men and women of God see how you disciple your wife, they will make a place for you among them. Like the angels praise God for the virtue that the church is walking in, men will praise you and look to you for leadership as they witness the virtue that your wife walks in.

The prophet Isaiah wrote of seeing the Lord sitting upon a throne, high and lifted up. Angels were flying around His throne, continually crying, "holy, holy, holy is the Lord God Almighty, the earth is full of His glory." The angels were praising God for His glory filling the earth.

Ephesians 3:10 reveals that the church is manifesting the manifold wisdom of God to the principalities and powers in heavenly places. Angels are observing the faithfulness of the many different members of the church and as they see the power of God in us, they give God the praise. The praises never stop in heaven because the angels always see glory; they cry, "The earth is full of Your glory". The elders are praising Jesus in the gates for the works that He has brought forth in His bride.

The husband of the virtuous woman of Proverbs 31 is known in the gates when he sits among the elders of the land. He commands respect; not by tooting his horn or acting showy, but by the works that he has brought forth. He has faithfully lead his wife into blessings, and to the place where she rules with God, and it shows all over her by the power that she walks in.

Giving Her Something Good to Study

Walking In The Law Of The Spirit

> She openeth her mouth with wisdom; and in her tongue is the law of kindness.

When people have faithfully pressed from glory to glory, flowing virtuously in many facets of their lives, they develop a rich understanding of grace. From the many stumbles and falls before attaining success, they learn how patient God has been with them. They understand that the people that have been waiting for them to come forth have been giving them grace when they missed the mark. People gave them grace to get up and keep coming forth. They themselves have learned to give grace, so that others who are stumbling can get up and keep coming forth.

As a Proverbs 31 man, while you are imparting virtue, you have to also impart the spirit of grace. By consistently exercising patience, in her not being there yet, and encouraging her to keep coming forth. You'll teach her the importance of giving grace to others. Not simply overlooking the shortcomings and faults of others, but patiently ministering grace to their lack. Grace is the substance that pushes emotions and rights and other things aside, by making room and giving opportunity for success. Grace is the longsuffering, gentle, good, and faithful side of kindness.

I have personally seen the effects of not ministering grace when dealing with shortcomings. I went through a season in my marriage, where I responded to my wife's shortcomings with the "law of sin and death". When she wasn't operating in something that I felt she should've been operating in I responded with condemnation. I consistently ministered the "what's the matter with you", "you should've done it this way", and "you just don't care". After a while I began to realize that my wife was shutting down to me, and withdrawing into her own world, away from me.

God began to convict me, causing my heart to break and soften. He showed me, how patient and longsuffering He is with me. How He hasn't bitten my head off when I obviously demonstrated that I'm not where I should be. He began to teach me how we, His people, are skilled at receiving His grace, but we squeeze out a gnat when it comes to giving grace. It's very sad how we, the church, are so quick to cut people off. Sometimes it seems like we've taken the portion of scripture where Jesus tells us to "shake off the dust of your feet", and we do it so expertly until it becomes our ministry. There is a time for shaking the dust from our feet, but it comes after, ministering much, the fruit of the Spirit.

The woman of Proverbs 31 was brought forth to a point where others knew that she spoke out of wisdom, and she ministered the law of kindness. As she was stumbling while pressing into God to be virtuous, someone gave her grace to keep getting up and keep coming forth. Whoever did it, and I believe it was her husband, gave her grace so consistently and powerfully that it made a life changing impact upon her, and now she walks in it too.

You Are My Epistle

By exercising yourself in the power that God has ordained you to walk in, you model a life that others, especially your wife, will be stirred to follow. When you consistently demonstrate the God kind of life, you'll make an impact that assuredly will leave an imprint, an imprint that will be known and read by men.

The principles of walking in divine virtue will be written in your wife's heart. It will be, written, by you consistently demonstrating virtue. You are writing a letter by sanctifying yourself to walking in virtue consistently and powerfully.

All is said and done that the word of God may be seen as well as heard upon the earth. The Bible teaches that Jesus Christ is the "word" of God, and that we are now the body of Christ. We are many parts or members making up the body of the "word" of God. When we wrestle with principalities and powers, it's to be loosed from the old, dead man and be more and more enmeshed in the word of God, so that we can take on and actually be manifested into that word. We are in the "press" to be made letters or epistles.

Giving Her Something Good to Study

The woman of Proverbs has been brought forth to the point where she is impacting the generation after her. "Her children arise up, and call her blessed." By the virtue that she walks in they are learning to discern what is blessed and what is not.

In 2 Cor. 3, the apostle Paul told the church at Corinth that they were his "epistle" or letter. He didn't have need of formal letters recommending him to men because his leadership and knowledge of God could be seen in his work, the people whom he brought forth, they were his letters.

You are my epistle. When you make a statement like that you really put yourself out there because when I see her I see your leadership abilities or lack thereof. If there's not much to her, there is not much to you. You might put on a good show, but your fruit will tell on you. If she's not resourceful, skillful or fruitful, it's because you couldn't put it there.

Whether it is good or bad, we all are making an impact and leaving an imprint. We are writing upon the hearts of the people with whom we have influence, and those epistles will be read. Whether your epistle is read as something virtuous or something fleshy depends upon your faithfulness. Ahab has to say, "Jezebel is my epistle". David has to say, "Michal, who doesn't understand my worship, is my epistle". Solomon has to say, "All of my unsaved wives are my epistles". The apostle Paul could proudly say of the church of Corinth, "You are my epistle", and God from heaven said of Jesus, "This is My beloved Son in whom I am well pleased. This is My "Word".

You too will have to say, "She is my epistle", but will you say it proudly or with shame? If you can't say it proudly, it would be wise of you to examine to what purpose you are sanctifying yourself. 1Cor 11:17 tells us that "The woman is the glory of the man", but that glory has to be imparted and brought forth.

Remember, it is no longer simply about you being anointed and walking in power. Now it's about your leadership abilities being honed to the point where you can lead someone who has been ordained to follow you to the place that exemplifies what is in you.

Please direct all comments, inquiries, and
requests for bookings to
van_brown@live.com

Participate in my discussion forum at www.proverbs31man.net where you can also read some of my favorite excerpts from **The Revelation of the Proverbs 31 Man** and order more books.

www.ingramcontent.com/pod-product-compliance
Lightning Source LLC
Chambersburg PA
CBHW060342080526
44584CB00013B/882